"SILVER SHA~~~~~ of the Moonlit Soul"

+++

POETIC AWAKENING

C.K. FORD

To: Quez

May your Gifts and Positivity
ALWAYS create place, space, and
opportunity for You. You are doing
amazing things, so stay focused
in ALL that you
do!

CK FORD Media

www.CKFord.Online

Peace and
Blessings,

C.K. Ford

" Silver Shadows of the Moonlit Soul" by: C.K. FORD

Published by: **C.K. Ford Media:**

Address: P.O. Box 44, Clarkston, GA 30021

Publication Imprint: CK\Ford#Media, United States

Website: **www.CKFord.Online**

Copyright © 2021 C.K. FORD Media

Cover Designed by Mr. James F. DiLuzio.

ISBN: 978-1-7361842-1-9 (Print / Paperback)

ISBN: 978-1-7361842-2-6 (E-Book)

Printed and Manufactured in the United States of America

First Edition

Acknowledgements:

To the Almighty Divine, I give honor and gratitude for the project as a whole. By way of Spirit, I live, move, and have my being of past, present, and future.

I dedicate this body of work to all of the people, places, and experiences from which I have received deeper insights into this journey called life. The gifts to be able to see beyond what is visible to the naked eyes, the acuity of hearing that which is unspoken is not only an art of antiquity- yet an enormous responsibility for which I have been chosen. I shall diligently carry this mantle of Spirit with grace and thanksgiving.

To those who have been partakers and contributors along the way, and in the junctures that our paths have either collided or intersected, I pray that the impact and deposits made in your lives has produced a great harvest.

Unto all those who came before me now abiding in The Great Cloud Witnesses- my ancestors, forebearers, friends, and family- both biological and Spiritual alike — thank you all for paving the way and laying the foundation, while making your mark upon humanity for others to share their Truth.

Namaste' and Ase'

Table of Contents

PREFACE

Come and take a walk with me through the many twists, bends, curves, triumphs, and epiphanies of LIFE — my Life by way of extensive Poetic Works and Messages as the deep calls out unto the depths. This compilation of writings spans over twenty years. A personification of Truth in the form of anthology… complete with dates that each piece was penned. It is my sincere hope that each reader is able to find themselves somewhere in the pages of this body of work, that it my resonate with you from the core of your being.

Some of the pieces in this body of work may seem "Other Worldly" — as if someone else is speaking to you, speaking to and through me. Precisely! When you listen attentively, you shall HEAR that which resonates with you from beyond places unknown, yet somehow familiar on a level not easily articulated. Each writing / message included in the pages of this book was specifically chosen to speak directly to the heart and soul of various subject matters--- The Essence of Life: a chronology of sorts as seen and heard through the spirit of a Poet. Be inspired, agitated, elevated, and moved towards living your life to the fullest. And so it Begins… one day at a time, Starting NOW !!! Thank you for traveling with me, a beautiful adventure awaits you….

"AIR-BRUSHED SUSPENSION"

Filtering through this--- ABYSS called a Soul.

And sorting out all those UNTOLD,

Truths so difficult to escape,

And should not still plague and ACHE...

The Psyche of all done and said-

As **Flashbacks** that somehow cloud the mind with

RED! ! !

And former realities that thought to be Dead,

Rush forward to greet or wretch the spirit into,

Proverbial twists of pretzel-like Complexities...

While chartered uncertainty of investments,

Did not liquidate to tangible amenities,

That flourish in the houses of the **<u>SURFACE RICH.</u>**

Yet beyond this crucial system glitch,

Required much more time and energy to fix,

Then could have ever been contemplated.

What the hell happened???!!

Question of the century and rightfully so,

And knowing that no easy Philosophies,

Can polish over the cracks and bruises,

Of the once *smooth* exterior.

Once GREEN with naivete,

Now GRAY with bewilderment,

And beyond reproach where deep within still lives,

The VISION of: SYNCHRONICITY & RECIPROCITY so rare that,

Even the auctioneer bids on that:

Kind of passion which is such an anomaly…

Yet who dares to dream this *LOUD*?!

In surround sound so clear,

And imagining being there,

Just for a fleeting moment until,

The present politely beckons Haste,

Though truly not a waste...

To venture into the familiar realm of the

UNKNOWN,

Yet fondly known of as HOME,

In the heart of the Unconventional

ARTISTS whose greatest- Inspiration

was the LOVE of the one Now--

Far away...

But as close as memories that dwell deep into,

Hues only treasured by the

IN- lookers, not the Onlookers!!!!!!!!

Written Friday, 26 April 2002 @ 1215 Hrs.

"ARCHED SANCTUM"

Crystal Blues and Perilous dues pair off,

To investigate the woes of time...

When all else failed,

Moments of truth unveiled,

Those oh so unpopular Causes and Effects,

While every other aspect,

That went unnoticed escaped into the night,

Without recourse of Dawn,

The radiance of Sunlight bypassed the longing of,

Those whom desired insight into places unknown,

And forthcoming...

As the trees danced to their favorite song,

Melodies strummed through the winds and rains,

Hummed all praises again and again,

Not a single cue missed-

Eternal graciousness and Faithfulness,

Yielding to meet-

Creatures of all kinds,

Regardless the shape, form, or normalcy of Actions,

Intentions, Emotions, Devotions,

Minor Infractions and Malfunctions!

Leave nothing to chance or happenstance,

To ever be rendered void,

Even in Silence, much can be heard through,

The bitter cold of winter- whether in the Night Sky,

There be fireworks of July,

Or Snowflakes searching for pillars of warmth,

Amidst the storms of December...

< Written: Friday, 15 October 3004 @ 1645 Hrs.>

<u>Billowed Symphony</u>

Blanketed with inner quiet,

Make way for all those unresolved things,

To surface and be reckoned with.

Listening to the stillness of the sunrise,

Summons even the Haughty and "Wise" to stand at ATTENTION,

Because one is forced to recognize,

That the world is not all about him / her,

Or some fancy whim décor' of Fluff,

Whereas, compared to the Majesty of the swift raindrops,

The woes of this very life,

Is it simply just the makings of all small stuff?

Hearkening the Conscience,

Though a remarkable feat,

Can drive even the most brilliant of minds,

To the brink of sheer Insanity!

Order and Priority,

Compete for their rightful place,

And Simplicity can humble,

Even the most embellished Noble in Grace!

Pure LOVE, without selfish intent and desires,

Channels, transcends, and quenches the mightiest of Fires…

Inescapable Character, though draped in Laughter,

Masks itself from prying eyes,

Of Hatred and Disaster.

Affording a sneak peek into the depths that reach,

Beyond the shallow plateaus of:

Those somehow notorious "All-time LOWS" !!

<Written : Tuesday, 23 July 2002 @ 1205 Hrs.>

"Canopy with Holes"

What more could be said,

About a LOVE Shared,

That has tied the SOUL into knots,

Since long before any IF's and BUT's,

Were ever to be considered?

Yet somehow, even now,

The very breath that keeps one alive,

Seems to be stifled in the midst,

Of every fleeting thought,

Of what was, wasn't, has been, could, or could not have been--

In the mirage of **Sanity** or *Insanity-*

And recalling that THIS Love,

Never made sense anyway...

Especially to everyone else!

Expressions through scattered prose,

And deep within the **wounded** spirit,

Is a silent cry: heard only at night,

Though the small voice inside,

Saying that everything will be alright...

However, the struggle between the mind and heart:

Is a never- ending rhapsody of Fire and Ice:

What is one man's Purgatory?

Is still yet another's Paradise!

Hold on to whatever infuses STRENGTH!

Regardless of how weak it makes all others THINK:

You are!

Besides, there is uniqueness to the enigma,

In not knowing how far and how long,

One would go, just for a Love,

That surpasses ALL Boundaries...

< Written: Sunday, 07 July 2002 / 1745 Hrs .>

"CONFETTI MENAGERIE"

Transition, Preconceived Positions-

Does not mean what it really seems… to be,

As changes in the betterment of the broken-hearted,

And stillness promotes a quiet too *Intense.*

And soon departed, to be Deciphered by:

The Shallow pools of Irony and Fate…

While costly mistakes can build,

Character in Synchronicity of:

Utter Disillusionment, Faithfulness, and Futility!

Who was that running through the rain screaming:

"WHAT ABOUT ME !!??"

Misplaced loyalties and jumbled priorities,

Deem the recognizable Aloof and Strong,

Though no one else heard the upbeat waltz,

That hummed of Long-Suffering-

Yet, tranquility rises,

As that one despised, covert strategy,

Quickly overthrows the pains and woes…

Predisposed from that which has long ago passed,

And could not Last through the:

Monsoon Season!

Though that jaded moon cast LIGHT upon,

The *Hidden Room,*

While primordial truths unveiled the proper use...

Of what was only meant for fading reasons,

Through pointless rhyme,

Transcends the time of that which is:

Not so Ever Lasting...

But far beyond reproach of the Diligent Coach,

While reaching into the depths that collapse,

The lifeboats that were inaptly Left Behind...

< Written: Wednesday, 29 January 2003 >

"CROSSED STITCHED FRENZY "

When the hurt takes root,

And carries on to--- the point where-

We Dare.... Not approach the pain to,

Embrace the scars of the Soul,

For as we grow old...

Time stands still for no one!

Navigating the high seas, with no compass or map,

Torrid and FIERCE, the **LIES** we tell Ourselves,

To ease back into who we are supposed to be:

SOCIALLY ACCEPTABLE!!!

A rock for all- Standing TALL-

The deafening SILENCES of those walking by...

As weeping prolongs the midnight hour-

Does joy truly come in the morning?

As the aches are gone,

Our memory is still....

LONG-SU FFERING!

Forgiveness surely a hard pill to swallow,

Careful not to allow anyone too close!

Pride is deadly, and so is revenge-

Some hit the *Bottom* slowly,

As they Binge-

To drown out what really happened...

"But *VENGEANCE* is Mine"- saith THE **Lord**.

At the point of no return,

The message buried beneath the ruins,

As the treasures tucked away-

And strategically hidden from the hands,

Of those- who **Raped, pilfered, and pillaged**,

The once fertile land!

Back up and analyze-

The agendas of the " SLICK"

For we shall be exalted from those **Labels**,

Stamped: *MISFIT*!

Once branded on the Soul,

Many think they KNOW,

Through enigma behind the eyes- the **REAL TRUTH**,

Has *NEVER* been told!!!

<Written: Saturday, 24 March 2001>

-

"DELAYED SURRENDER"

At the surface of those Dreams,

Hidden Realities unravel,

Heard you calling out to me in that:

Subconscious state,

Arresting me in Spirit,

But why not in the waking hours?

Grasped my hand and told me to wait,

Stand still, you pleaded,

Because this time you were here to stay...

Tugging at my soul, though we are worlds apart,

Why Now?! After all these years,

Do you cry out to me and say that you will...

Never Leave?

You walked away long ago,

So, I thought you were Long GONE!

Where is the end of this complex fate?

Hesitate... or reach into the unknown?

Far too overwhelming to just toss aside,

After, Destruction plays counterpart,

To **Arrogance and Pride**!!

Don't know what you want from me now,

But it shall all be made clear,

As your spirit cries out and beckons me near-

The whereabouts in primordial doubt,

Nevertheless, through the dreams,

One hears: Far more than was ever meant to be revealed!

< Written: Monday, 12 July 2004 @ 1225 Hrs.>

"DESERT FOLIAGE"

Anxiously reaching and fearlessly teaching,

Along the stay and for one more day,

Don't know if to hold fast or run away,

From all that did not' t feel right,

But feelings can be such deceptive devices,

Sacrifices and Proverbial Paradise,

Tend to get twisted and entwined,

While gruesome Truths,

Have somehow escaped youth,

Dwindled into this supposed "Adult Life"...

As one bought the ticket,

Someone else paid the price!

HURRAY!! Now, Let's hear it for the BIG SPENDERS!

However it goes,

No one even knows,

The where's, when's, or why's:

Of the too tough brutes against-

The Oh So Ten de r fledglings,

But to what shall I render-

This semi-faithful service?

Giving and Living...

Hand in hand-

Who has seen the Promised Land?

Flowing with all that milk and honey?

Might seem funny,

Especially when there ain't no money,

To make things happen the way they should,

Don't hear anybody laughing yet.

Just to be Found when no one was around,

Is this not ironic anyway?

If at all pliable,

Who would be deemed liable,

For those that fell through the cracks.

While their mothers Lacked ·

The know-how of societal woes,

To pull them from the throes of:

Fates too horrific to tell...

Even if screamed from the mountaintops,

Who would dare listen on any given day?

Waking up to the call of Clarity,

Brings such rampant disparity,

Among they that just wanted to- Do the "Right Thing"...

By everyone else except himself!

Who dares to dust off that book…

After it is removed from that high shelf?

Way back in the corner of the room--

Makes one wonder who is Listening,

Even if you are not making a sound...

<Written: Wednesday, 26 February 2003 / 1845 Hrs. >

"DETOURED RETROSPECT"

Is a Good-bye for good?

Or a Farewell beyond compare?

Yet sometimes, it all seems too complex,

Through instrumental devices, and not for Sacrifices,

Of the heart are much too short,

In supply and demand…

While conventional contraband is:

Highly Overrated!

Contemplation of those Loved Ones,

Who drifted away from the ties of Unity,

And Loyalties that lie deep within,

For those friends that have not been seen in years,

Yet somehow Spiritually Bound-

And Reconnected though Lost AND Found,

In hidden realities known as Dreams,

And the sheer Awakening of those Untapped Means,

That were supposed to be a part of that *Past Life.*

No matter what the cost of all those that are gone,

Wil one day find themselves back together,

In an illogical assortment of proposed fates,

Yet commonalities that did not vanish,

Because who we were, is still a part of us now,

Where we have been, wherever we go,

There will always be a tomorrow,

To be unlocked by that---

Dastardly yesterday of Faith.

Hopes, Dreams, and uncommon Fidelity…

That bind and intertwine the hearts of they who still Remember!

Those when's, how's, who's,

And all that never could be!

However, this is far from being the end of the story.

Did the end not justify the inconspicuous connections?

As surely as I live and breathe,

Bypassing all Unbelievable Means of Wisdom

Leaving no place or space for rejection!

<Written: Saturday, 21 September 2002
/ 1450 Hrs.>

"DUBIOUS PATCHWORK"

In the quiet of tl1e still night,

When all things sleep,

Filtering through all those hidden realities,

Each neatly tucked away in its own private place,

Clearly seeing each Face that has come and gone,

Yet in the Soul, still lives on,

Never forgotten because impacts that will not release,

The Lessons bought and paid for through bleeding Heart.

And Tears,

Intermingled with treasures shared, but somehow- Lost-

Track of how it was, maybe the quest for the Key...

Is far more wretched tl1an what was to be the cost,

Of the FEELINGS themselves ...

Reciprocity of a RARE kind,

Unwinding of the Soul,

Slowly spin11ing beyond control,

Dare not to relinquish the tales of Old,

Days in the Sacred Realm of Friendships,

Yielding desires, for temptations creep in,

Far too potent just to give in- And Lose the Moments of then,

When whatever could never have been...

Surfaces AGAIN,

But too Late, as it would seem,

Though regrets have No Place,

As we learn from our MISTAKES,

Because is Anything truly ever,

As it Should, Could, or Would not Be?

Mysteries that PROTECT us from ourselves,

Yet Sometimes worth more than the WEIGHT…

In WEALTH.

< Written: Sunday, 29 July 2001 >

"ELEVATE FROM the VALLEY"

The Have's and Have Not's,

Wants and Needs,

All shall come in Time,

To they who so Good Seed,

Harvest is bountiful,

Though Laborers are few,

Prosperity not in vain,

The path less traveled,

By the ones who shall remain,

NAMELESS…

And only lived to do the *Right Thing,*

By everyone else, except him / herself!

Good deeds that make the Ordinary,

Become *Extraordinary,*

Kings and Queens, labeled by their own strife,

Are not treasured,

Until they are gone and gone,

Those that Loved them,

Still Live on, to tell their stories,

Of how the races were won.

Physical strength not measured,

Yet, **FAITH** kept them **STRONG!**

Reasons change throughout each Season,

Dry and barren sands,

Across the *Distant Lands*,

Ranis quench the Earth,

New Life springs forth,

Evolution of what has always been,

From what never was before!

The Oceans part, tides rise and fall,

How could there not be **WATER in the Wilderness,**

While others were shown the *Promised Land?*

From small seeds,

Large vines grow,

Cultivate the Young,

For the paths that they should go.

Lead not to Mislead,

In all that is done and said,

Poor are not those who have none to spare,

Poorest are those who forgot how to **CARE!!**

Empty Hearts,

Robbed Souls,

No love in Life,

But pockets full of Gold,

Yet still Spiritually **_BANKRUPT!!_**

Is there a witness?

Or has all departed???

Changes we meet,

People on the street,

Every Season has Purpose,

But not every rhyme has Reason.

Peace from Within,

Brings forth New Perspective,

Pray for those souls that are Lost and Alone,

In hope to find Direction…

<Written: Friday, 22 May 1999 >

"EMPHATIC DRAMATICS"

Contortionists of *Agony* scampered through the streets,

Undefeated Madness, fueled by Insanity,

Just stopped to feed the souls in need,

Over-extended the patience and kindness of Heart,

Now bleeding internally puddles of Grief and Fire,

What about all those tears of Ice,

That escaped the charms of twisted desires.

No matter what took place,

At that wrongful time and space,

No one ever stopped to consider the *Graceful Hopeful-*

Treasures covered over by the ashes of Disrupted Loyalties…

Even though the Royalties are now in *Default.*

The lowest bidder,

The price too high for the "supposed winner",

The runner-up who lost out in that warped game of:

Dishonor and Shame!

Does anyone ever remember the names…?

Of those who ransomed off the Princess of Hearts?

Yet apart from it all,

The Loser did not fall,

But walked away with the counterfeit goods-

When the *Rarest of Jewels* were passed over,

For the sake of imitation relations!

Ironic scenario, unworthy at best,

Discord obviously ravaged fruits,

That was plundered by the Pests…

And the vision tarnished, unfinished, and ridiculed,

Perhaps the foolish are deemed so,

Because they played by the rules-

And would accept no half-hearted Substitutes…

Yet somehow displaced by those characters of:

ILL REPUTE!!

< Written: Wednesday, 03 December 2003 >

"Enchanted Rapture: The Man behind the Mask"

Beneath the Surface,

So many layers of Depth,

Intellectual Power,

Spiritual Wealth,

Perhaps, a method beyond the Madness,

But not seen with the naked eye,

Halted in my tracks,

In Wonderment of,

WHO IS THAT MAN?

Though often misunderstood,

The book not to be judged by its cover,

Strikes **FEAR** in some,

Inspires **AWE** in others,

If not recognized to be a friend,

No chances of being the Lover.

Educated to meet the challenges,

Every day of his life,

Poignant and Wise,

Back off and Analyze,

No half-stepping allowed-

Yet truly on the Rise.

Come Strong and Fierce,

Or dare not come at all,

Weaklings admire from afar,

For he is: **The Essence of a Strong BLACK MAN!**

The brother has what it takes,

To make all STAND TALL-

For any given occasion,

Though he clearly states:

No Applause or Praises Necessary, for I know who I AM!

Through Motivation without ulterior Motive,

Curiosity and a meeting of the minds,

Cultivated and nurtured Friendship,

From the sparks of two of a kind.

Never mistake what is seen,

For being all that there is.

Look behind the Eyes,

And to much surprise,

Inner Beauty and Warmth,

Not shown to all,

The Mystery now solved!!

WHO IS THAT MAN??

Only those spiritually connected,

Are provided the privilege to understand,

My hat goes off,

And I grant a quick bow to my Friend:

Essence and Grace,

Of yet the oh so Magnificent **Powerful BLACK MAN!!!**

< _Written: Friday, 23 July 1999_ >

"EYES in the STORM"

Utter Confusion, though it may seem,

Not withheld from the brink of this thing,

Somehow not perceived as it is so,

Though in the midst of it all,

One should already **Know** -- that there is Nothing,

That can be seen that will not change.

May sound Strange,

But direct transcription from the Higher Powers that be,

Behind the PEACE and DOMINION of the *Hierarchy* that Reigns
Supreme...

The clouds dissipate,

As lack of hesitation prevails,

Through another time and place,

But still not Erased from the Soul,

Yet **GOLD** is on the border,

Of horizons unknown,

To those without a Voice,

Did not Rejoice when it *Rained*,

And wallowed in the temporal pains,

Of a false sense of Reality!

Built houses made of glass,

And dwelt with those of **Under-Class Spirits**...

Impoverished by lack of Revelation Knowledge and utter Non-Belief!

Restoration Breakthroughs,

For the days of New,

Arrives on the shore,

Of what was no more,

Then a passing tribulation,

Soon made subject to Exaltation…

Freedom abounds,

And without a mark or sound,

IT WA OVER,

Before it ever truly began,

Anywhere else other than,

A ferocious *Battle within the MIND!!*

< Written: Monday, 07 January 2002 / 1100 Hrs.>

"FROM BONDAGE to FREEDOM"

Can one reach out to Touch what no one else can see?

Do we define our Lives, or is Life Sculptured--

By those that we meet?

Explore the Possibilities, Reach for the SKIES,

Surely, we shall be rendered empty-handed,

If fear overwhelms, we lose Faith, and then we never tried!

Limitations are imposed Shackles deemed necessary to Control,

Seize the Keys, Break the Chains that Bind,

FREE YOUR MIND!!!

Sighs of Relief?

Discontentment or Disbelief?

Throw away Conformity,

Allow your Creativity to Soar!!

Can on fully understand what has yet to be defined?

Explanations become crystal clear with Time…

Opportunity does not happen by chance,

We must unlock the Doors of Inner Consciousness-

Depths channel Energies that unleash Power,

Dare to Explore,

The inward chambers of the Soul,

If not for a single moment,

So quickly passes the Hours…

< Written: Thursday, 04 December 1997

≥

"GLORY DAYS"

Darkness beyond that of Time, even before the Sun,

It seemed the light of day never to come,

Too far away, somehow remembering how One-

Ever **Survived...**

Plights of war, supposedly for FREEDOM's sake,

Yet the *Real Battle* sometimes still aches the mind.

To what expense is this Liberty and Justice anyway?

Which certainly does not come without the highest of costs,

While too tired to stay awake, yet too frightened to sleep,

As the QUESTIONS always linger deep,

Are we on target, or did we get lost?

Somewhere in the center of that hell forbidden place called,

The Middle East!!

As seen strictly through the eyes of a Soldier.

And there is absolutely nothing glorious or exciting about
showering.

OUTDOORS!!!

With choppers and missiles zooming overhead,

While the pilots attempt to fly as LOW as they can possibly go,

Hanging out the helicopters by a rope,

Just hoping to snap a few photos,

Of a girl simply trying to get clean,

Through any means—NECESSARY…

Even though its only 45 degrees!

Blue and shivering is just NOT that sexy.

"Thanks for the **Thrill Pics** Babe- You are Looking oh so Good- they said-

And you casually flip them off and yell: Don't end up DEAD- Today!!!…

Who is the Ally and who is FOE?

Yet to be determined as we all know,

It all depends on what year it is,

And how deep of a hole we have dug ourselves into—

Policing and minding everybody else's business on Foreign Soils…

So much left to be desired,

Through the blood, sweat, and tears,

Even those that come back Alive,

Distinctly remember years—

That was senselessly condensed to:

The Shields and Desert Storms to feel like Perdition-

In what is to be relived as the Longest-

Eight months of a Strife---

Turning 21 in the middle of a war zone…

Just another day in the Life… of a Soldier!!!

How is that for Glory and Valor??

At least I came back "alive", well *Somewhat.*

Quite "Interesting" being the only woman--

Deployed into combat zone with a team of Thirteen Men...

Not sure what is more brutal, the missiles, sirens, night air raids,

Or the Good-Old Boy REDNECK Regime—

Oh, we are NOT sorry for saying Racist Shit to you,

You do NOT get to file a Formal Complaint-

You are damned *lucky* that "We Allowed"

{{ *SOMEBODY LIKE YOU* }}

To work / serve in a 'Prestigious Field' Like This Anyway—

As they spat their snuff tobacco juice into the same tin cup,

That was used for Drinking GIN out of earlier.

Do You go thinking about Making any Waves,

Or we will have to See about--

Yanking your Security Clearance Away!!

They said: It just will not "look right" if we do not keep,

AT LEAST ONE BLACK PERSON ON DAY SHIFT!!!

And NO! We Refuse to APPROVE YOU for transfer-

To night shift or assign you to a different department to Escape...

From- the Asshole Senior Sergeant who snatched you by the arm,

Then drew back his fist to hit you because...

He does not like your attitude, calling you an Uppity Black Bitch—

A combat boot to the shins and the knee out to do the trick-

The element of Surprise and Pain, he let go really quick...

Got his just desserts when my Faithful Friend and Brother *Roy*
stepped in-

And took "the mighty Quinn's" ass to task-

Got in the guy's face-

Grabbed him by the collar and shoved him so hard-

Nearly knocking him to the ground!

And said "If You EVER –

Touch my friend again, your very next breath WILL BE YOUR
LAST!!

And your wife will be collecting Survivors Death Benefits...

No one has ever seen the world until,

The government has been your travel agency,

And your compass, terrain maps, and grid coordinates

Serve as your Tour Guide,

Flying in the belly of that C-5 Cargo Plane,

Lodged between pallets of tactical equipment and Humvees--

Hey, come hang with the *Elite Soldiers* and be all you can be:

The great adventures: Tent dwelling, Sandstorms, Bad Food,
Parasites,

Sleepless nights,

Did the Chemical Alarms just go off again?

Oh, that's just the SCUD Missile incoming right across the fence!

Shit gets real when a limousine with 4 Turban clad locals attempted,

To kidnap you in broad daylight—

After all, they said, they were just looking for a New Wife--

To add to their Harem!

You are just a Woman, and YOU have no say so--

NO RIGHTS in Our Country…

Maybe we can PAY 20 bags of Silver and 2 Camels.

To have those guards on Patrol to just Look the Other Way, they say…

If you happen to be female, do NOT go ANYWHERE alone,

Especially--at Night,

Not even to the Outdoor Bathrooms… Predators are on the Prowl!

Oh, did you think I was referring to "OUR Enemies"?

NO, Beware of that Military Policeman STALKER,

Courtesy of "The Dragons' Lair"

You thought they were there—

To "Protect, Defend, and Serve??---

Not *HOLD YOU HOSTAGE AT GUN-POINT*

All because you have NO INTEREST in wanting to *date* them!!!

Someone had to tell the story,

So why not me?

Duty calls, no stalling,

Your twelve- hour shift just came around Again,

And they all say: *THANK YOU FOR YOUR SERVICE*:

And THIS is what happens amongst those…

Ranks of Honor and Valor--

Cloaked in the bloody Days of
GLORY!!!

Diesel Fuel and Testosterone Drives this Train—

Suck it up, Stand Tall, and

MARCH on Like a Good SOLDIER--

A I R B O R N E!!!

HOO-RAH !!

< *Written: Sunday, 02 December 2001* >

"INTANGIBLE FAITH"

Dedications of the heart, we seek not to Find,

Though the **BATTERED** in Spirit, somehow fell behind.

The works of The ALMIGHTY be not in vain,

And we shall not lack any good thing!

After the former and latter rains,

Washes the injured souls clean.

Revived and restored, a **NEW** Creation born,

Through *Naked Eyes-* he who is forlorn,

Emerges from the Storm,

And Rejoices amidst of pure hell knocking down the door!

We know not of the Lights in Store...

Behind the silence- a NEW Day dawns,

As if they had never been on-

The face of This Earth!

Yet, descended from *Another World-*

Clothed in **Goodness, Mercy, Grace, and Love,**

Never to be **Cold, Lonely, or WORN-**

Another Day!

For all has passed away...

Renewing of the mind brings about change,

Though in the **<u>FAMILIAR-</u>** it may sound strange,

And we know not where and why we go,

But shall surely recognize those who are sent-

Bearing the Burdens, Pains, and Dents,

To be repaired by HE who went-

To the cross to die for US,

Through the Blood is JUSTICE!

Deep in the hearts of they who Believe,

Free of Worry, Poverty, and Disease,

Resurrection comes by Faith of the Dead,

And Due Season shall be restored again,

Not lacking any good thing!

Peace reigns and **Dominion** in our hands-

Regardless of the Opinions of feeble-minded man,

It is done; finished- and rightfully so,

As we call all that be not- as it was before!

The spoken works of the **Most High God,**

Shall be exalted throughout the land…

Give *Praise and Thanksgiving,*

As we ALL shout **Hallelujah and AMEN !!!**

<u>*< Written: Friday, 23 March 2001 >*</u>

"JOURNEYS of FATE"

People come and go,

Passing through our lives,

Enriching our Spiritual Growth,

All too often, friends lose touch,

But are they every *really* gone?

Deep in our memories, the LOVE lives on.

Think back on those treasured moments recklessly spent,

When days melted into sunsets,

Then nights into Sunrise.

Tough times seemed relentless, unwavering,

Unlike the brisk winter breezes,

Sweeping away those yesteryears,

Here for the moment, then Away we all went,

Traveling down the many diverse paths to find our own ways,

As we journey back in nostalgia and smile,

We cling to in our hearts,

Those small pieces of Yesterday,

Tomorrows much too close,

"Back in the Day", so very far away.

Time wasted, preciously gone —

Ture friends are Forever,

Though out of touch, but never out of mind.

Bonds we shared from *The Good Old Days* so rare in kind.

Remember with your Heart,

Reminisce in your Soul,

Seek and you shall find,

Treasures of Gold,

Brothers and Sisters in Spirit,

Through distance and circumstance departed,

Yet never too far behind.

Timeless Friendships,

Yesterdays, Tomorrows, Forever-

Linked through memories,

Blessed by God,

Real friends remain,

Strong unti8l the end.

Surviving the scrapes,

Overcoming the pains,

Only the strong survive the hurts,

In the cold, cruel world of Life.

After the Storms,

Trails of Sunshine,

Paint the path to Rainbows…

If only Time would just stand still !!!

Perhaps for a few moments, anyway.

Memories that linger,

Like balloons in the wind,

Journeys of Fate does have no end.

Don't know if we will ever see each other again,

Yet, I bid ye' Farewells to those **Fair-Weather Friends.**

< Written: Friday, 20 February 1998 >

"KALEIDOSCOPE RAIN"

Finding PEACE from with the Broken Pieces,

Of Wreckage and Chaos of Days Past,

Foreshadowing the Liberty and Joy,

Seemingly out of grasp...

A deep sight, expelling those hurts and trauma not seen,

With the naked eyes, Opening WIDE,

The Hearts that birth out untapped TRUTHS from deep within...

The Why's and When's of this or that,

Escaped the Reality of all those Then's, Now's, and How's,

Ever increasing Mercy and Grace,

Even without clear Understanding...

Just simply accepting of what was-

Regardless of how treacherous and tumultuous-

The who's, should's, and could nots were...

Surrendering to the Bigger Plans,

And Purposes that appear so out of reach,

As the Divine Mistress WISDOM teaches-

That no matter where we go, there we are,

And Right NOW (TODAY)-

Restarts the Clock to:

NEW BEGINNINGS- seeking out,

Those who will Embrace and receive,

The offerings of Celebration and Worthiness,

Through Unconventional Means…

Of simply BEING IN THE NOW-

While ALLOWING all other Impromptu Incidentals-

To fall by the wayside,

Dying out to make way for:

The Newness and Renovations-

Resurrected and Restored,

Creations of Splendor in Untarnished Forms!

< Written: Tuesday, 15 January 2019 >

"LET THERE BE LIGHT"

Seek and Ye' shall find,

Or so it has been said,

Look Forward; for the days that are behind,

Has long since passed.

Embrace the Yesterdays, Careful not to cling too tight.

For therein lies the Keys that unlock the doors to the Future,

Walk towards the Light!!

Though only Darkness may be visible,

The rains downpour for what seems to be Years,

As one Evolves through Acceptance,

The Sun brings forth a New Day to the Earth,

Alas, Pure Light…

Just on the other side of Darkness,

The Rain is gone, washing away all Fears…

Sometimes Light is not visible because our eyes are closed,

Although lost in Darkness far too long,

The spark of Light which burns from Within,

Our Shelter from the Cold,

Perseverance makes us Strong,

And we Fiercely hang On,

To the Songs of the Wind…

< Written: Wednesday, 12 November 1997 >

"LORD in the TIGHT PLACES"

Expansions and Extensions of my Solemn Grace I

AM GOD no matter what, even in your "tight places" …

Regardless of appearances sake,

Feelings of Hopelessness, Turmoil, and Despair,

I AM with you ALWAYS-

Even when it seems like no one else cares!

I AM either LORD over all or Creator of none,

The victories are not granted to the weak and defeated,

Yet the races are won by those who overcome,

The deep hurts, pains, adversity of unthinkable sorts

As My People surrender all to Me,

Through the relinquishing of Self-Reliance and Headstrong
Defiance,

While lifting up their hands withholding nothing,

They shall be set on Divine Course and certainly not miss the mark!

For I alone am God Almighty that Nurtures, Supplies, Vindicates,
and Redeems…

What then shall YOU SAY unto and about all these things?

Because My Presence is before and with you,

You shall not be overtaken,

While being uplifted by My Wind underneath your wings.

In these "Overcoming Processes", I am developing your Fortitude,
Power and Progress,

So, fail not to take notes and utilize what you have learned.

Though the crippled, maimed, and bound- those suffering all around,

Have not lost the race until they are silenced by disgrace,

While refusing to allow the Sound of My Praises

To be RELEASED in the midst of the struggles and storms.

I AM the Lord Almighty: Creator of the great and the small,

I came not for one, but welcome ALL into Salvation,

I am the Great God over night and day,

So, dare not waste crucial moments on rehearsing and nursing past regrets and mistakes.

Shout HALLELUJAH! for I have not left you all alone,

ARISE from the ashes and emerge as the Dove,

Reach for Me… I am not far,

The spark within that causes you to Sing when you feel like crying!

I AM GOD Right Now and never has that changed,

REJOICE in the midst of the wildfires and pains,

For I AM WATER that quenches the parched barren lands,

Although for many seasons there has been no rain!

Well done to those who not only HEAR, yet avail themselves with:

Humble, Willing Hearts to Obey- because they LOVE ME…

For I AM LORD especially in your "Tight Places" and …

HELP IS ON THE WAY!

And as of THIS VERY DAY-

Holdfast to My Promises, asking for the Grace to Just BELIEVE

Broken in and obedient to follow my direction and instructions,
THEN RECEIVE the Harvests…

I have not abandoned you or left you in the wilderness to die,

So, ARISE and RECEIVE all that I have decreed,

As you do likewise, I shall establish YOUR

Proclamations as you have simply.

BELIEVED ME at my Word,

Accepting those "Tight Places" as prime –

Opportunities, Resurrection of Greatness, and Creative Abilities…

For Direction, Growth, Expansion, Extension in New Dimensions
and Unchartered Territories…

You do not know and cannot see all that I AM working out behind
the scenes,

YET, PEACE BE STILL unto your weary worn soul,

For I have always had a plan,

Listen to MY VOICE, the Write the Vision and Make it Plain,

For I have placed My Power in your hands,

To Touch, Inspire, and Bless those who are clueless and do not
understand…

I have made the ways possible, opened the Doors…

So GO FORTH in your Faith in ME by the Grace and Authority as
you wear My Name,

You are neither forsaken nor forgotten…

I AM the LORD ALMIGHTY, and you are NOW in Receipt of:

My Spectacular Glory…

Simply say THANK YOU LORD, YES and AMEN…

because you Trust Me, I accept this Mantle of Responsibility!

Shout HALLELUJAH, for others are Set Free-

by the Power of Your Testimony.

This story is not over, for New Beginnings arrive at Lightning Speed-

in the Here and NOW!

Receive NOW this outpouring of Mercy and Fresh Grace,

WHOLENESS, COMPLETION, and Expansion.

The essential, fortifying growth came about in these darkest hours!

Lament NO MORE!

ARISE! ARISE!!!

Rejoice in Me- as I AM in you and with you…

I, the LORD ALMIGHTY Am The

GOD of and IN your *"tight places."*

< Written: November 17, 2009 / 2126 Hrs. >

"*LOST In* **BONDAGE**"

So, you say that you don't like Me,

For my views are too Powerful for You,

Resolution: Don't slither around trying…

To Pick my brain and

Ask me what I think.

If you are too weak to accept My TRUTH,

Perhaps radical, though you could NEVER understand,

What it is to walk in the shoes of:

An Educated Black Woman.

Who are you to try to control ME and cause me pain---?

ABSOLUTELY NOBODY!!!

Prejudices come in all shapes and forms,

Whispering about those who refuse to Conform,

To your standards of acceptability-

For those who don't quite "Fit the Norms".

Prejudicial constructs are Ignorance Based,

Though ignorance can be taught,

Only if some let down their guard,

Airs of Pretension,

To receive the education that their

Inheritances could not afford,

HOW DARE YOU pre-judge ME !!

Contrary to those oh so "Popular" Beliefs,

Al of "WE PEOPLE" are Not-

Murderers, Liars, Drug Dealers,

Prostitutes, Welfare Recipients,

Nor **Common Thieves !!**

The First Peoples of Humanity,

From which all other Races were spawn,

Nurturing- Indicative of our Nature,

Created to Excel,

Yet STOLEN from Our Motherland,

Chained, beaten, and thrown, and Transported,

Through the gates of HELL,

Still yet, we Endured, Adapted, Prospered, and OVERCAME-

So much atrocity- while being,

Extracted of our most precious resources,

Now Do Tell,

Who gives a damn about Your Perception of OUR TRUTH ?

You say that the playing field is now *EQUAL*,

And we have been paid our just rewards,

Instead of being granted-

Those *Forty Acres and a Mule,*

We were forced into Enslavement,

While being overpowered into working your ancestors,

Forty acres or MORE of Cotton, Indigo, Sugarcane, Tobacco-

While being dragged behind a Mule,

OR those Ford / Chevy PICKUP TRUCKS !!

However, regardless of the weather —

You tout and shout about :

Justice and Liberty for ALL !!

Perhaps, I simply cannot recall which Lie,

About FREEDOM you are yelling from the rooftops about —

Or what hill you are willing to Die Upon to get your point across.

But WAIT, who is that poor soul,

Swinging from the tree?

By a Rope around his / her neck, that is…

Down in the heart of Dixieland,

Possibly somewhere in Alabama, Louisiana, or

Mississippi…

After Four Hundred or more Years of Bondage-

And through our *"Civil Liberties", Public Discourse,*

The struggles and fights to be SEEN as FREE People,

Such a pity it is, I feel sorry for You,

Because YOU DO NOT even Really KNOW ME !!!

Too bad you are not Free In your Mind —

Rendered Blind with Ambiguity…

Just to recognize that there is a Different Truth,

That Lies beneath the skin tones that you see —

After all, we stand tall in various shades and tones,

Some of us fair with dark Red Hair,

Green Eyes and WISE —

The lines became blurred —

From all that Rape and Oppression, that is,

As you are unashamedly locked inside the darkness,

And bewilderment of those ties that bind-

Imprinted on the Minds of those unable to See —

Beyond the stigmas and Mirrors-

That shines the Light on what true Empathy and Compassion-

Beyond Comparisons were meant to Be…

Written: Tuesday, 27 April 1999 >

"MAHOGANY SHADOWS"

Prior to Elevation and Exaltations,

The *"Due Process"* is far more consuming,

Then the Promised Harvest —

That lies somewhere in the midst of,

Those bitter tragedies and pain,

And intently racking the brain with:

Confusion and lack of focus…

While no JUSTICE seen by the *Righteous,*

To smooth away the days of hardship spent.

Simply hoping to be whisked away,

Into a crisp mountain breeze,

And blowing LEAVES the mind of:

Considerable ease,

Because traipsing through that Field,

Of Flowers is a little bit of Paradise…

To the soul that has seen far too much strife!

In not even old enough to refer to the past,

As quote the good old days in quote in life, yet.

Anyhow, anyway-

Why not NOW?

For the rewards are stored,

Until the **HEALING,**

Simplifies those bruised egos in lies,

That swallows one alive and all that is past.

And still able to laugh at:

How all is not as bad as it used to be,

While the only thing that would quiet,

The stormed soul is:

Peace of Mind and Sanity.

Yet, the hardest to achieve,

And by all means,

Hidden from the scavengers capitalized,

Who only wanted to pilfer the ruins, of those brutal years,

That are not lost,

But will be replenished,

One Thousand- fold of the original cost!

Imagine how easy it would be to just,

Toss it all off

And bask in the freedom,

That was both sold and bought by,

Almighty who sees all, heard all,

While restoring those Broken Souls,

When the very fire that somehow burned others,

Chiseled off bits and pieces to produce pure GOLD,

Yet, the half of this story has never been told!

<*Written:* Friday, 05 July 2002 @ 1438 Hours.>

"MELODY of TREASURED PLACES"

In the quietness dawn, while still yet dark and cold,

And thinking back on those days of old,

Yet anticipating your embrace,

Captivated by your smile,

As my soul desperately awaits,

The caressing warmth of those,

Familiar and missed gentle touches,

Knowing all too well that it has been way too long...

yet, deep from within, we never let go,

Of all that we knew and held sacred from the time before,

Whereas, who would have dared to dream this loud?!!

While blocking others out of those places,

That only we shared,

And shutting out all intruders, predators, and prying eyes,

Regardless of the reasons or changes in the Seasons,

And no one else knew either How or Why,

We would end up back at the beginning,

Of what would be our own fairy tale paradise...

What was then, is still so now, Undeniable connections,

That never died and failed to subside,

Yet somehow was reborn through,

This mystical Soul-Tie that lives on,

Although seemingly hidden and buried alive in years past,

The destiny of the delightfully inconceivable:

LOVE that knows no boundaries, distances, or end,

For what once was, pulled us back to the place,

Never lost or somewhat forgotten!

<u>Written: Thursday, 17 November 2005></u>

"Microscopic View of the Big "NOT SO EASY"

Been so long since that quiet night song,

Of nothing but the wind and the crickets chirping,

Way down in that small town Suburb of "Red Stick"

In the Heart of the South… formally known as Louisiana…

When my friend Anna and I, would sit in the middle of the narrow-

Rarely traveled street, around midnight on weekends…

In front of my house on the hill, or on her grandfather's porch,

Just dreaming of the days when We would escape all!

Yet, the madness and Mediocrity of that boring, simplistic world.

Kindly reference by others as HOME…

Yet, in MY Scope of Consciousness,

Just Anywhere's- Ville : Dead center of nowhere- small town USA!

Back in the place where my mind in spirit was far too broad,

To simply just seemingly waste away,

When there was a whole big world out there,

Beckoning to me to taste, enjoy, and take it by storm…

Don't never quite fit into the quote, unquote norm of,

The ideals of the content type,

Regardless of what they said,

Never really believed. The Hype.,

And knew that there was so much more for me-

Than what I could visibly SEE!

Outside my bedroom window,

And quaint neighborhood…

Without concern, my dream seemed good enough,

To Take Me Out of that place,

Where I would discover all things,

That I used to read about while lost in encyclopedias.,

And cautioned about, by many Elders.

Years later, in journeys around the globe,

One recognizes that no matter where you go,

A part of who you are, is deeply rooted,

In the soil that you. First sprouted from.

Yet, outgrew much too quickly for the comforts of:

Those who were bypassed, allowed the world to-

Pass them by, or, strangely enough, withered away and died.,

Into their yesteryears,

While still raising their glasses and bottles in honor,

Taking a long stiff drink to all those who are no longer here!!

< Written: Friday, 02 August 2002 / 0025 Hrs.>

"NEUTRAL ESTABLISHMENT"

Took a deep sigh,

Just to try to stay alive,

While inside, the bruised ego,

Lies underneath the heart,

Yet worlds apart-- from anything ever seen or imagined.

Eyes that witnessed too much strife,

When before the other life,

Distant memories greet the now,

And somehow, seems just a bit too familiar!

Somewhere off the beaten path,

Laughter took a trip,

Far away from the peculiar...

No one ever noticed it was raining outside!

And all those holes in the roof,

Drawing in the Aloof

Who just wanted to keep from drowning--

Where is the lifeguard when you need him anyway??

Let this be the Reason,

For the snow in July...

Frozen sunrays glisten,

While Faith forgot to Listen,

To the warnings of Danger,

As weakening and ever- present ANGER grew closer,

Who neglected to lock the door??

Silence louder than horrific screams,

Danced into the room as if it owned the place,

What a tremendous taste... of capitalize reality!

Everyone knows that *Green Eyes* don't cry-

Been categorized as the strong, quiet type...

But by what means??

Don't believe all that hype!

Pardon me, Stranger.

Need to borrow a Cup of Sanity...

Apologies, extended- did not know that,

You two were all tapped out!

Where is the storm in the midst of this drought??

And finally, it RAINS-

Perhaps, it will replenish the displaced sphere,

That is heavy on mileage,

Somehow, Light in YEARS!

< Written: Saturday, 01 March 2003 >

"OPAQUE DAYBREAK"

Don't know why, on such a day as this,

If everything appearing plausible,

Really exists- in the Natural Form...

Of Charms, proper grooming, social accept abilities,

And the fading thing called Honesty.

Being propelled by situations,

Blocked in by limitations that others,

Set forth for thee,

However, Regardless of the weather,

People and circumstances are quite:

Flaky and Fickle. You see...

Why ask why?- When the **TRUTH** is such a Rarity,

That all involved weave themselves into-

Complexities,

Which cannot even be sorted out by:

A *Rocket Scientist,*

And "New Age" Phenomena is merely a Hoax,

To mask the ancient vices of:

Witchcraft and alchemy!!

Funny thing is: when the problem is diagnosed

The symptoms are placated,

But no one Funny thing is when the problem is diagnosed

The symptoms are placated, but no one out the cure.

The audience is not laughing yet,

In the time well spent with that psychiatrist,

Costing a small Fortune.

While losing that sudden Allure…

And missing the mark. On those professional charts-

When all along, Purity of Heart and Integrity,

Were supposed to be FREE!!

Caught up by the subtlety of it all,

By vacuuming out the dust, from the tiny crevices of the heart,

And shaking off the cobwebs from:

Inspirations bought...

Through the hard lessons that Reality taught!

Suddenly marching forward without:

Regret or doubts,

Is the passionate, fierce spirit,

That was buried underneath,

Those mountains of. Grief, abuse is,

And the crippling Anxieties!

But now! A Priceless, Treasured, **WORK of ART !!!**

< Written: Friday, 12 July 2002 / 1840 Hrs. >

"PAINTED PERCEPTION"

If the heart could paint a picture of our lives many Endeavors,

Would that picture whisper a thousand thoughts?

Cast light on dreams that are Sleeping Realities, only at night,

Or mend Broken Spirits who once believed in "*Forever*"??

Reflections of yesteryears. That same what never end,

Sites of wonderment, enchantment, disbelief,

Nostalgia sweeps in,

Not so long ago, Or "Way Back When"??

If the eyes are the capitalize windows and capitalize mirrors of the souls,

Why sometimes so difficult to see,

How ART reflects Truth in Life,

Painting paths of fine strokes in Hues of Light,

Illuminated and only imagined,

Leaving behind Clarity,

In ***Brilliant Colors !!***

Art is reflective of the souls who create,

While the beauty of life sometimes,

Breed contempt and hate,

Focus: Look through the window from both sides,

Love too much? Love too little? Or, love too late.??

Only within and for Self. can we ever really decide.

< Written: Friday, 07 November 1997 >

"PARTITIONED ARRIVALS"

Chipping away at those unsealed cracks,

That were supposed to be mast over-

On reachable, Untouchable, yet pushback...

Denied in hidden until this new season emerged,

Changes or continuous? .... Perhaps on the verge of,

Something that was missed, while spiraling beyond the abyss.

Deep Inside the silence of things Profound,

Sanctity of Solitude resounding--

Amidst the Thunder and Stars.

The time did not halt,

The dams that were built to protect from the floods,

Somehow in the distance is hearing the Teardrops of Blood,

Broke all barriers and transcended the Impossible.,

Then the odds not only turned favorable,

But tangible beyond Recognition!

Excavation of Sacred Lands,

Yields treasures unknown and before long,

The beauty is unmatched, glowing with brilliance,

Far too prevalent for those naked eyes, and Forlorn hearts!

Do not be forever awakened, enamored, softened, Enlightened-

In heightened expectancy of the delightfully strange,

Beyond comparison of the stable or deranged...

Carefully examined through *Cautious Eyes*,

What was once deemed as "Foolish Notions"

Are now confounding those ***Worldly Wise***!!

After the rise and fall of the tides,

Piece creeps into vacation for a while,

Then clarity seeks. Capitalize companions and capitalize friends,

Those Once Insidious **VISIONS** birth,

The manifestations of Glory, Splendor and

TOTAL SURRENDER,

While beckoning the Lost unto the Light Of:

That Welcoming Newfound Home!!!

< Written: Monday, 05 July 2004 / 0245 Hrs.>

"PECULIAR DIMENSIONS"

In the midst of this oh so Troublesome Day,

Weariness and despair go nowhere,

Yet deeply plagues the mind,

However, in due time,

Ain't nobody mad but the enemy anyway…

What then shall one say to all these things??

If L- should I goes before me,

Then the way has already been made,

And nothing is as it seems,

Through the birthing of **DREAM,**

Manifestation only breaks free, when there are growing pains,

And recognize — as the Due Seasons come with time,

Shall be viewed as light afflictions anyway,

Prepare for the downpour of Rains!!

Pressing in and pushing forth brings new direction,

Tell me why and when-

Is it not the issue at hand,

Yet, strictly the emotional and mental perception??

Speak light into the dark places,

For this too shall pass

And when in need-

Just ASK: **JEHOVAH JIREH**-

The Almighty Provider...

Who is Supplier of **ALL** needs,

According to Divine Riches and **GLORY**!!

One must believe before it is received,

An rejoice even before the blessing arrives,

For intellectualism both **denies** and **defies**,

Divine Revelation Knowledge,

And Reckless Faith waters the soul,

Infuses impartation of the _Godly Wise_!!

< Written: Wednesday, 16 January 2002 / 1305 Hours

"Personification of Inscribed Fury"

My Dearest Sister…Why do you have the "Blues"?

Are you going through changes with that Brother,

Who is so unworthy of you?

Tired lines, Jealously, Possessive, Two-timing, Lying,

Constantly robbing you of your Joy…

Are you not worthy of a King, instead of a peasant boy?

Sweep the cobwebs off you Charms,

You have stored away behind the scenes,

Polish your Crown, Adorn you Temple,

Position yourself to become BLESSED…

With all your hopes and dreams!

After all, YOU are a **LADY of INDEPENDENT MEANS.**

Set a fire for the trash,

While asking GOD to restore your Happiness.

Leave behind in the Ashes-

"Mr. I'm SO BROKE, cannot afford to Pay Attention,

Can you loan me two dollars so I can buy a clue?

Baby, YOU KNOW that I LOVE YOU though"!!!

Now, is not that about enough…

To make you want to Scream and Holler?!!

Sure, you have thought long and hard,

Please do realize that you are selling yourself short,

Do not block your blessings,

And always remember that,

Any tree that bears bad fruit,

Should be chopped down and thrown into the Fire!

No matter how you slice the fruit,

It will always taste BITTER…

Not trying to tell you how to run your life,

You have already been delivered from-

Heartache and Strife…

Though you may not want to be alone,

You have clearly been shown-

How GOD blesses those who have been chosen as GOD's Own…

Do not allow anyone to drag you down,

Or take you back to the fortresses,

That you have already been set free from.

Toss the Copper and hold out for your GOLD !

You will not receive your Divine Inheritance,

When you continue to allow thieves to Rob Your SOUL !

Weakness of the flesh may be,

Sometimes hard to shake,

Your future is far too precious-

All that snake to indulge in no more of your pleasures,

When you decide to Walk Away !!

Have FAITH and take HEART,

In whom YOU ARE…

YOU are a Daughter of Sarah and Abraham!

So, GOD will not lead you astray,

The KING that awaits You,

Is only a blink and flicker away-

When you choose to Obey the leading of SPIRIT!

You are a Magnificent Artwork,

That reflects the beauty of GOD in Creation!

Hold out for that Virtuous Man of Valor and Godly Character,

For whom YOU shall be Respected, Celebrated, and Appreciated!

If a Man is not first processed and prepared to reflect the Image-

Of Divine LOVE through GOD-

He is unworthy of a The Divine Priestess Daughters—

For only the Righteous, Humble, Pure at Heart shall inherit-

The PROMISED LAND,

Now may the Transformed and Redeemed of the LORD ALMIGHTY-

Take a Stand, while rendering emphatic praise, shouts of Joy,

And Boldly Proclaim HALLELUAH and AMEN !!!

< Written: Wednesday, 22 September 1999 >

"PROJECTIVE EPIPHANY"

What LIES within the heart of man?

Who has always been told he CANNOT,

Do anything capital RI GHT or capital WRONG,

Four in this Song... And Dance,

No room for chance, but change,

Peculiar or strange,

Time is of the very essence,

To overcome those that had come over, to the well to drink--

And perhaps to sit and think,

As thirst and hunger is what breaks down barriers,

That Social Constructs and Economy established...

Long before the man ever discovered,

That he would starve no more!

While all caps FAITH kept him fed,

Though in his head- he looked to,

The Left and to the Right,

Without friend or foe insight,

Something Greater than he, sustained his very LIFE!

Not all things are of a means,

To breakdown the soul,

But implemented to break the souls out from BONDAGE called,

SELF- RELIANCE.

As defiance nibbles away like a parasite,

To hinder Destiny, VISION, and capital Dreams...

Funny it seems- how those very things,

That were meant to destroy,

Catapulted vessels into *"New Territory"*.

Never to be seen or heard before,

Preconceived ideologies,

Grieves and dampens the vision,

While blocking and squashing any cost-

The beacon of Light that seeks out the Lost...

And BROKEN.

Cash in those chips off the shoulders,

And strips away,

Capital OVERPOSURES of Smokes-screens and Mirrors,

Cloaks and Daggers-

As we rise above ALL those:

SELF -IMPOSED

Limps and Staggers!

< Written: Tuesday, 03 December 2001 / 0629 Hrs.>

"Prophetic Exclamation of the New World Order"

Busy people all around,

Noises on the streets,

No silence to be found.

The Lost and the Homeless,

What is *Liberty* anyway??

Life, Freedom, Happiness,

The pursuit of the coveted *All American Pie,*

The capital R ICH space walk on water,

While the Poor drown below,

The innocent suffers most,

As the children fall through the cracks,

While their desperate mothers Lacked,

A little part of everyone's soul shall surely die,

While the very foundation was built on:

The **Backs of SLAVES**, that is…

Somehow the scars never healed,

From the force behind the **Lashes**.

In the land of the Affluent,

Flowing with Milk and Honey,

No one should be without Food,

Or a Home to call their Own!

Inflation on the rise,

Religious Enterprise,

Since when did worshipping **The Almighty**,

Become the "trendy" thing to do?

Drug dealers, "God Sent" Leaders,

Cruise the boulevards in their **WHITE Cadillacs,**

While the "**Poor Working Class**",

Scramble to live from paycheck to paycheck,

Yet, they ALL aim to be:

POLITICALLY CORRECT !!

Somebody is walking around with their purses and pockets "Phat"!

Prayer banned from schools,

Metal detectors at every door,

Wide- I'd empty stairs,

Outcasts and clicks,

As disgruntled capital MISFITS,

Bomb the workplace and subways-

Gives new meaning to the phrase:

"**Faith No More**"!!

The world is not coming to an end,

Armageddon is already here to stay,

Do not need to go to hell,

Because Purgatory is coming to us;

As depletion of the ozone layers,

Burns holes in our lungs,

Where is the justice??

It has long gone out the window in a handbasket!

Marriage, surely a thing of the past,

shagging up and divorce,

Or thing of the new revolution:

Capital AIDS, Child Pornography, Teenage Pregnancy-

No one has the solution!!

Wake up all!

Salvation calls,

Pick up the Divine Guidance instead of diet pills,

The map to paradise is easy to read,

Divine intervention can fulfill all needs!

The soul is what weighs a ton of gold,

Not the size of the frame that houses,

All those Idiosyncrasies!

Who said that Prayer does not change anything?

What capital God are you praying to??

And then, what are you praying for?

As simplistic as it seems,

Though not transparent,

Since when did living a *"good life'* -

Start and end with the green dollar bills,

Or whatever the prized Currency…

While whittling away of Virtue, Impeccable Character,

Integrity, Steadfast Morality?

As we walk through the Valleys,

Of the Shadows of capital DEATH,

Knocking outside the front door,

Praise God the **Almighty** for all that was provisioned,

And the blessings that were stored up for us.

At this time,

It is so hard to recognize,

Not what vehicle or motive one drives home,

But what drives those souls,

Beyond the Darkness of those who are Blind,

While Tearfully Declaring-

Shouts from the Bus Stops, Rooftops, and the Street Corners of:

FAITH NO MORE !!

< Written: Thursday, 26 August 1999 >

"REALITY ETCHED in STONE"

Deep in the heart so scarred with pains,

Strength prevails, and life goes on,

Humming bittersweet melodies,

Singing quiet songs,

Wonder how she made it?

No one really knows...

Days gone by, fierce and strong,

Inhale too much,

Exhale too little,

Hurts, fears, joy and laughter,

Here today, but who knows for how long!!

Play with the hand you are dealt,

Learn from it, or burned from it,

Yet still Life goes on...

Don't things rarely go your way,

No time to cry and moan, duty calls: wake up!

Bills do, pockets empty,

Full time Self- Sacrifice for the kids,

Job unfulfilling, not paying what nearly you are worth,

Just do what is Necessary,

Sooner or later, it has to get better!

The only thing reliable is-

Changes in the Weather.

Trust and Faith in God,

Surely must have paved the way,

Survival of the fittest,

No one is promised one more day,

Do what you can with what you have,

And let us not forget to Pray.

With every turmoil and strife,

Inside Lies-- lessons to be learned,

Extract the moral,

Reject the hurt.

Seek out the Reality, in Light of the Dream,

To discover only what you so deeply Yearn...

For time stands still for no one,

Day after day, accumulates two years,

Whether we have Lived, Love has passed us by,

Or we long ago have perished,

Life still goes on...

And somewhere in the depths of the heart,

She still sings a quiet song,

Listen closely, as her Rhythm catches on...

As Love breathes life into the souls of the Lost,

We may not get what we pay for,

Yet, must always pay for what we get,

Do you have enough Substance of Spirit --?

To afford THIS Cost??

< Written: Monday, 07 September 1998 >

"SCENIC ADAPTERS"

Streetlights and Hindsight circumvent,

Those things that were destined to destroy...

Just as a toy is overturned,

And crushed into ruins,

Instead of repair, it is replaced,

As haste beckons waste through,

The FOLLY and disgrace of carnality,

In the face of ADVERSITY,

And perversion in all grotesque forms,

Simply fails to edify mankind or GOD.

Deep from within the bowels of hell,

Arose they who were supposed to be WISE...

Now, do tell?!

By worldly standards, that is.

And by chance tapped into capital DIVINE things-

Hidden from humanity,

For those whose Purpose and Plans are now one with:

"The Great I AM" !

Drinking from the cisterns and wells of:

Revelation Kingdom knowledge,

While Dominion is reestablished again,

And even *after* the fall,

The falters and fleshly calls,

Are hereby diminished for once and for all!

Stirring the pot and watching it boil over,

The heat turned up hotter than the norm,

Just to make the Nobles Evolve into their chosen form-

Majestic PRINCES and QUEENS of *Humble* Charms…

To add here no more to that lowly living of capital EXCESS,

Deemed fit of the world,

And the callings and precepts bent,

Those that were all spent out of:

Patience, Temperance, Self- Indulgence, and Indignation!

And before the enemy's very eyes,

Those who were Made Subject to Divine Exaltations-

While standing in the center of the *"Promised Land"*!

< Written: Saturday, 20 July 2002 / 1000 Hrs.>

"Scrambled FOLLY"

Dreams and Schemes both,

Color the means of what is to be birthed Someday,

Though some ways are grander than others,

Decisions of whom to keep as friends,

And who to toss aside like worthless lovers,

Stand to be a million to one odds and ins.

And how to determine who WINS,

Where no prize to be won except:

Those far too great to be captured with *NAKED EYES*,

Or touch of the fingertips,

And on the very edge of the capital LIPS,

Are numerous words and few **ACCOMPLISHMENTS**,

Of *Significant Value…*

Yet worth their weight in Pure **GOLD,**

The lessons to be told to those who,

Quest after knowledge, but discover,

Truth through slightly peculiar *mechanisms,*

Not befitting of a **Sleuth,**

In the midst of that "To Do List",

How much really gets done anyway?

Or is actually planned by the everlasting,

FOOL-PROOF MAN!

Caught up in the wealth held by:

The Mediocre Hands and benefit nobody except,

The **EGOS** that are continually…

Fed by the drops of *bloodshed,*

And at the end of the day,

Still able to rest because they are-

CONSCIENCE DEAD!!

To all that did not adhere to the game,

When the rules were not clear to anyone except,

That *Master of FATE,*

Called *HATE and DISCORD…*

When the only thing that was required was-

To Worship, Honor, and Love the **LORD!**

And treat thy brother / sister as they would themselves,

In the Sharing of thy Goodness, MERCY, and **WEALTH,**

With the poor and needy who could himself…

Yet transgressions, unlike iniquities are clothed in GRACE,

And does not bury us Alive,

Long before we Die.

For they who are now Lowly, shall one day,

Reign on High,

As God Almighty is surely standing by!

And we shall understand it better as each Star,

Is aptly **Positioned** for LIGHT in the Darkness,

Of the Night Sky.

Now is the time to wipe off the mud,

And remove all blinders from those once **Naked Eyes!!!**

< Written: Friday, 26 April 2002 / 1315 Hours >

"SCULPTURED ABSTRACTIONS"

Anticipation of those places someday to be seen,

Yet to be determined as only in Dreams,

Of days when the Memories dissipate into the mist of-

Silences...

Daring to share or unlock the chambers beyond the **Soul,**

And far too many times Never to be Told:

Truths unrevealed,

To the naked eyes,

Tears of past hurts rush forward to meet,

The **REALISM,**

In the hearts,

Never to depart from the depths within-

When all that was **Lost,**

But somehow Unforgotten,

Bid the Cost of Payments Owed...

Debts of Emotional Enigma bought,

Though weighed and calculated by-

Numbers, places, times, and faces,

That never quite added up-

To the total of *Simplistic Difficulties* that got in the way,

Of Mystical, Majestic Houses,

Built from the Grains of Sand!

Untapped treasures-

Somehow missed the banks,

Embarking the *Promised Land.*

How can this be?

And thus concludes those traced Masquerades,

While safely harboring this-

Drenched Soliloquy…

< Written: Tuesday, 22 January 2002 / 12:00 Hours >

"SOLILOQUY TRANSPOSED"

Almost forgot how time escaped,

Nostalgia comes knocking,

Twice as Loud as REALITY,

Of what once was, so very long ago,

Or perhaps mistaken for Another time and place,

In the Depths of the mind,

Trails of Sadness, Madness, Laughter, and Pain,

Making way for the Birth of-

Creation and Inspiration in spite,

Of what the Years left Behind,

Fears that attempted to bind,

The Heights of POTENTIAL...

Dare to Dream the Impossible!

For many deem it not plausible,

Yet, within the Spirit, unsheltered territory,

Desperately drawing closer,

To grasp all that is Predestined...

In the blink of an eye, what could be,

Evolves into the NOW, then through what was,

Melted away fears of missing those who:

Touched, Caressed, Plundered, and Wrenched-

The SOUL,

Of every possible Emotion known and imagined!

As weakness dissipates,

Power prevails through Eternal Strength Self-Contained,

And who would there be to blame,

If the Memories and Dreams were all that was Left,

Spliced between those chambers of Pain?

Delicately masked behind the walls of Prose,

Many think they See clearly,

Yet, Nobody REALLY **Knows!**

< Written: Sunday, 29 July 2001 >

"SPLICED REFRACTION"

As dawn awakened in the Golden Violet song,

And all listened attentively,

As the horizon strummed on-

Commanding the attention of everyone,

That happened to buy a ticket to the starlets show,

One time performance, unlike any before...

Behold! The splendor of the new seasons came,

Suddenly the rain stopped in the midst of the storm,

And without obvious reason,

The territory changed,

Into magnificent landscape that was yet strange.

Though anticipated long ago,

A single beat not lost unable to be revamped,

While out in the wilderness, arose a temporary camp,

Utilized to gather the value predisposed,

Thoroughly untapped from the land of old,

Inside the soul unfolded:

Dimensions of the unseen and not to be told!!

Trampling through the black sands,

On the brink of the seashore,

And tossed into the volcanoes appearing dormant and still,

Moreover, stroking the throbbing egos of fates unknown-

To the heart that ceased to dare,

Envisions beyond compare,

As the brilliance climbed the height,

And reluctantly took flight,

Out, over, and around,

The barriers and sounds,

Of those transgressions of Spirit,

Which sought to cripple the bound!!

Meanwhile, painstakingly freed,

By breaking the confines off the capital ingenuity,

Indeed! Streams of Consciousness hastening,

The call two claims for once and for all...

< Written: Sunday, 01 June 2003 / 0645 Hours >

"STEPPING STONES and OBSTACLES"

Can you fly?

Not on an airplane, or drugs that get you High.

Understanding is where it all starts,

From Beginning to End, from the depths of the Soul,

With every beat of the heart,

Someone is always there, watching over us all!

Hoping that the right decisions are always made,

Utilizing Instinct,

Guiding the way to Enlightenment,

If somehow, we get lost,

Or sidetracked out in the Wilderness,

Never be afraid to stop where you are,

To ask for directions.

Listen carefully, then execute!

The rest of your life could be determined,

By that single moment in time...

Ask for the Definitive,

As to the Purpose for which you were born,

When weariness lingers like the darkest of clouds,

Do not despair, we must go on.

For the Rainbow is not visible in all its Splendor,

Until *after the storm*.

The race is not won by the swift,

But unto those who have Endured.

Although each generation has its own plight, the struggles remain,

We must not lose sight, that our lives do not belong to us,

But to the ones who made us who we are.

Through experiences in relationships,

We are molded like clay from the earth,

Rare, genuine artifacts and pottery,

Etched with fine lines from:

Heartache, Losses, Laughter, Disappointments,

From being touched, treasured, and measured,

By those faithful onlookers in the Audience,

Set in slow motion, performed on the Stages decorated for-

Orchestrated Symphonies of Life.

Angels appear in the rarest of forms,

Often presenting themselves,

As normal beings we encounter each day,

To guide us and hold our hands, along the way,

Sometimes Friend, Kin, and even Foe,

The more we Listen, the more we shall Know!

Close your eyes,

Reach for the Sky,

We are not capital BLIND if we simply cannot SEE.

We are rendered Blind, Mute, Deaf, and Lame,

Where there is no FAITH,

And we choose not to seek the Truth.

For Divine Truth is worth mountains of Gold!

Do as you please,

But always listen to what you are told.

Extract the Positivity from the Truth,

Expelled the negativity,

For it preys up on the Weak,

While robbing the Soul,

Leaving one helpless,

Stranded in the Cold,

To no one except The Almighty,

Should you relinquish all Control!!!

< Written: Tuesday, 18 May 1999 >

"SUBLIME FUTILITY"

Those STORMS that arise,

And where we fall,

Though to and fro' – no one to call…

For all alone in the midst of the Silence does ring,

How shall I lack any the necessary things?

As Home clings to the bones and flesh,

Blankets of Warmth-

Yet still not undressed, in a Fresh PERSPECTIVE !!!

Time covers and mends the cracks throughout the Soul,

The clock ticks fiercely, wandering into,

Those old Moments when All else seems LOST,

Sanity of Madness… the truth bids the Cost,

Of the price paid through the bleeding heart and tears,

Only to escape the Enigma of Years,

Missed or Stolen from the lyrics of songs,

Whosoever glorified that which is *Long-Suffering?*

As the hours scatter through heartbreak and fame,

Cease All FIRE, as this very game,

Proves to be **FATAL!!**

Depleting the Spirit just a little too much,

Where the tangibility of a simple touch,

Blows away the fragile second of-

When everything that should have been-

SAID vanishes into thin air!

Then again, are there any such comforts- Beyond the Despair??

< Written: Tuesday, 22 May 2001 >

"The Dawning of the THIRD Day"

Wandering back through the journey, inside the loss souls,

The search for Restoration, feverishly growing Cold,

Then, Great Mercies of Salvation –

Covers for shelter to those without a home.

The quest for belonging, that almost escape the reach,

Listening to the voices: as the apostles and prophets teach,

Of goodness, wealth, and glory, so plentiful to us all,

By grace Redeemed, a New Order of the Third Day, yet after the FALL!

Come Ye' the Obedient of the Lord,

With Bonds of Unity- we stand of One Accord.

Speak Light into the darkness,

Prior to each VICTORY comes the Storm,

But THIS TOO SHALL PASS !

Thanksgiving and Praise to exalt the presence-

Of the Most- High God, Arise- as Children of **The King**,

Knowing our True Identity and Purpose that we were created for!

Thus, we shall not lack any good thing!

Through the blood- the price for freedom was long ago paid!

Those faithful in little the little things shall be Blessed with much,

Sow the good seeds of Love and Trust.

Reap the harvest- of FAVOR!

Shalom: nothing missing, nothing broken,

For this day, the LORD Almighty has SPOKEN-

And so, IT SHALL BE DONE!!

< Written: 21 February 2001 >

"TRAIL of TEARS"

Laughter, sorrow, joy and pain,

Who dares open the door,

Inviting hurt again??

Here today, then gone tomorrow,

What happened to those promises of Forever?

Standing a miss what once was,

False impressions, commitments, *Young Love...*

Sometimes one-sided and Conditional.

One who gives and one who takes,

Destruction and chaos,

Is what makes,

Foundations crumbled down,

Whatever happened to those fabled *Happily Ever-After's*?

Or is Someone out *"Painting the Town"-*

RED with Blood,

Or GREEN with Envy,

Together for eternity,

Flourishes only in Fairytales…

Dreams soon come to waste,

Silence creeps in, no joy to be heard,

Whispers sound like screams,

Going through the motions,

When there are no words, to describe the pain,

Left behind, when the pieces are shattered,

And cannot be glued back together again!

Not every broken thing can be fixed.

Perhaps therein lies a lesson to be learned

He said this, and she said that,

Dreadfully so, there are two broken hearts.

Where the hell do we go from here???!!!

Two must be snipped from the same fine cloth,

Carefully stitched together, so that no one can tear apart

The designs of the pattern,

That creates a coat of many colors,

Suited for King to be worn in all kinds of weather.

Divided in conquered,

The house then falls,

Trees will only grow strong and tall

If the roots are grounded deeply beneath the topsoil!

The love may not conquer and break the fall,

Where we are slack, the almighty sees all!

When there is faith, we are strong,

Every shelter that stands is not always a home...

Families with Love of God as Foundation-

Are never all alone…

For all of those who have Loved and Lost,

There comes a time to Pay the Cost

To be one's own boss,

For nobody else can be made to fill,

The voids of your Soul.

It is not always better to have than to hold.

God blesses those who seek with a Love of their very own!

Search for Salvation to fill the voids,

When all is gone and hope is lost,

There is nothing left for anyone else to take,

Replenish SELF first and foremost,

Gold or weights,

Let go, seek WISDOM,

But be conscious of the Cost,

The price that must be paid, when stripe is overcome,

We are blessed to prosper,

So that we can bless others,

Spare no expense!

Know your limitations and when to quit,

Everything broken is not meant to be fixed,

Recoup, regroup,

Choose the next one more carefully,

Just as we choose a new suit or dress,

One who not only seeks the Outward Appearances to Impress,

Yet, Empowered and Blessed in Wisdom-

Suited up in Fine Character befitting of Spirit of Soul,

Dignity and Self-Respect,

Are such treasures to Behold,

Grace that is with us even as we grow Old…

All that is bound together in the ties of humanity-

May NOT be- Equally Yoked by God Almighty —

So You've got to KNOW when to Let Go---

Without REGRETS…

< Written: Thursday, 24 June 1999 >

"TRIBUTARY of PEARLS"

Recognition of those untouchable truths,

Hidden from predators, protected by Youth...

Though in the here and now, *PARDONS* of Fate-

Or wait as a matter of formalities,

Set sail, yet in height and expectancy,

Never too late to reveal-

All that was withheld until the proper time and place,

Which brought about rapid change and secret travail!

After all else was purged and purified-

Those dauntless magical moments,

surfaced, resurfaced, then overthrew-

Everything and everyone they ever knew...

For therein lies those unexplained Life-Ties of the Soul,

Always arising, never subsiding from:

The Days of Old.

Where masquerades wants rolled the forefront,

Those primordial unfeigned elements,

Relented, and broke down all defenses!

And all done and said, the Scenic Trail,

Led to the inevitable, yet deemed for so long

As highly unlikely...

The years came and went, while fortitude and patience wove,

Intricate circles of Crossed Paths,

Into timeless devotion,

Never to be broken yet spoken of…

Only by those who swam against the Undercurrent,

And somehow **SURVIVED**, even **THRIVED**!

Then transitioned into that which was Predestined,

Long before they were ever alive,

And even Lifetimes over after they had died,

For the spirit knows no boundaries as,

Epiphany unfolds-

Leaving behind details to be deciphered

At some other point and place in Time…

< Written: Sunday, 25 June 2005 / 1742 Hours >

"TRIPPED WIRES of NIGHT"

Feeling your presence in the distance-

As I felt the distance of your presence,

Even when you were supposed to be

Near and oh so dear-

Although the years have come and gone,

The hurts lingered on...

Disillusioned by all that was, left unsaid- yet in secret, now you just go on,

Like none of it ever happened,

And WE were nothing more than a factor-

A minor casualty of war, in a battle that unfolded

Crashing into the sidelines- being hit by the shrapnel of deceit and lies...

What really gives- certainly not you!

Yet always taking every part of me, that you could

Leaving behind the Ashes of broken promises,

Of all those wish I would, should have's, and can not's-

At least not in this not at this time you said!

Borrowing from the reserves,

Though never returning anything but sorrows-

And the infamous disappearing acts-

When the untainted facts on matters of heart,

Somehow never came clean to truth untold,

Eventually exposed by way of deep searching,

Only to discover that –

Recovery is as painful as being trapped with the unknowingness

Of whether you ever really cared!

You should come with a permanent warning label.

Proceed with caution: Known to cause,

<u>Severe Injury and Systemic Shock!</u>

When in doubt, refrain from prolonged contact,

And unlimited exposure…

< Written: Sunday, 12 November 2017 >

"UNDEFINED QUEST"

Thinking back on days so long ago,

I still remember things that I really should know.

A life of many dark secrets,

Ghost lurking behind closed doors,

Embrace the yesterday's,

For tomorrows may come no more...

No one truly knows just what life has in store.

Pass edges trails into the sands of time,

Leaving scars of yesterday's behind,

Future beckons, present looks to past for insights,

In two days to come...

Unbroken cycles of timelessness,

Echoing in the wind.

Forget nothing:

Everyone encountered, even the bleakest face,

From Chaos emerges Order,

We know not the exact time or place

When everything familiar becomes a Distant Memory,

If remembered at all!!!

Summer quickly sinks into Fall,

Vanishing into thin air without a single trace...

Reality or dream?

Substance or waste??

Listen closely to the Spirit Voice Inside,

Focus intently,

Swallow your Pride,

Dream of ancient lands far and wide...

The world is so much more than what we readily see,

Right outside our own back door,

Where would you like to be?

Is there such a thing as destiny?

If so, then who holds the Keys,

Could we be the Master of our own Fate?

Or bound in states of Suspended Animation,

Through the Higher Powers that be??

< Written: Friday, 05 December 1997 >

"UNFAMILIAR TERRITORY"

He who justifies the mighty tales told,

Imparts the Impoverished ways of old,

And slowly anticipate the throne of Grace,

Boldly redeemed in the sanctity of Places-

Seen, heard, explored, implored,

By all who sought to *Grieve NO MORE*...

To whom shall the Favor be dispersed?

Through the Wisdom of Faith,

They who dare to Immerse-

Into the depths of the shores untold-

The breaking of day, then The Almighty said:

"BEHOLD ! For this day you must choose,

Your master of Fate; Stay on course and run YOUR race,

The swift shall not win,

But unto they who shall endure-

The Just Wealth and Gifts are Poured Into-

Those who are PURE at Heart!! "

Embark upon the Journey set forth,

Faith that marks the mighty and the tame,

As the Lame walked, the Mute talked,

And the DEAF heard!

The passing of silence called for:

A WORD... in Due Season!

For all that had been seen was more than,

What they undoubtedly saw...

No rewards rendered for Espionage and
Treason!

Written: Tuesday 05 March 2003 / 1930 Hours >

"VISION QUEST"

Listening to The Voice, Heed the call,

Who searches for the Souls after they Fall?

Restoration from Chaos… Determined or defined?

The Deaf: they dare not hear, the Lost or the Blind…

Yet, a Balanced Renewal emerges from a Silence,

Which is **LOUD** enough to Pierce the Beginning of Time!

Stop or proceed?! As caution grabs the WOUNDED of Heart,

That anxiously ponders Change-

Conformed, or Reformed?

Eyes that captivated the mightiest of mankind,

Though too often blinded from the Sparks behind the Pain,

In Seasons of drought, they meditated for RAIN

Yet unable to embrace the flood,

Which began as mere traces a single tear…

Someone lost their heart, though never found Love!

Whimsical or strategic?

The refreshing stream of ice,

Quickly melts away on borrowed time-

Evaporates before the breath of life,

Which could have molded a Flicker of Fire,

Into an Air-brushed Breathtaking Sunset

Or tiny Private Paradise…

< Written: Tuesday, 10 June 199 7 >

"Visual Revelation or Aimless imagination"

Snowflakes fall, wet cold, razor, silver or?

Where is the sunshine?

Unspoken thoughts, the truth untold,

Is it not better to have than to hold?

Cloudy or clarity? Perception Personified... Individualized!!!

Knowledge or uncertainty?

Sparks or Fire,

What is your heart's deepest Desire...?

Love, Passion, or Lust??

Love consumes, Passions Inspire,

Lust: temporary gratification, no substance required...

Emptiness ceases when self -appreciation surmounts,

External nourishment... Through Internal nurturing of the Soul--

Alas, **Serenity** unfolds!

If one is not whole while alone,

Only half still exist through loving another.

Do you *KNOW* who you are??

Or is your core existence defined through the **Eyes** of *Others*?

That Fearless Soul- the One who holds-

Their head high while standing Alone,

Touches the heart and finds their way home.

For HOME is where the heart is,

If the Spirit within never dies,

Lessons profoundly taught by asking:

"HOW", instead of *"Why"*??

< Written: Monday, 29 December 1997 >

"When STAINED GLASS WINDOWS Bleed"

Unbottling of the Soul from-

Those plagues and pains of old,

Releasing of horrendous Truths,

Never spoken, never told-

The screams that were buried alive, yet kept inside-

Hidden in an unmarked grave…

No voice given, no name, self-blame,

All the same whether day or night,

The fight of decades, lifetimes, generations past,

Cast many shadows and masks of:

Silences Profound!

Though if given way, time, space, place,

To LET GO if and when no one around…

Those blood curdling, time shattering-

Sounds from wounds so deep,

That set into motion: Slow beyond agonizing Death of sorts…

The kind where one functions, seemingly Alive-

Yet somehow seemingly missing the mark,

And never quite able to THRIVE!!!

Until that brutal, fateful Autumn Day of –

One November…

When the dams of hallowed Souls broke-

OPEN, unable to push back Surrender,

The uncorked screams of somewhere in the Beyond…

Erupted from the bowels of Creation,

Piercing the fibers of the Universe at Core-

Pain's voice spoke audibly,

To be SILENCED NO MORE!

Repressions, anxiety, grief,

FEAR, Sorrows, Supernatural Release!

As an underwater volcano Opens her chambers for lava-

Under Pressure to ESCAPE,

First Birthing destruction,

Then gave way to New Creation…

Healing over TIME; One Step, One Breath,

One Heartbeat, One Moment, ONE WORD…

Allowing space, place, and GRACE,

To guide every step of the way!

One more day, one more DREAM-

The nightmares that once terrorized,

Have now been tranquilized, paralyzed,

And put to a final SLEEP…

Meditation or Medication-

THERAPY: whatever works!

NO JUDGEMENT!!

Then, the SUNRISE Illuminated what had been dark before...

And for a brief moment-

I recognized and realized that,

Fear and sorrow had walked out the door,

So, I changed the locks, opened the windows to...

A NEW EXISTANCE of REALITY,

Standing aside for the Fresh Winds of change...

To Blow through like,

And Ocean Breeze after a Cleansing RAIN!

And YOU also can Begin AGAIN,

And AGAIN, while Dancing on the Edge of the Wind,

Start with a Smile, then a Laugh,

A walk in the Sun, then a Brisk Run,

A small Celebration for a Party of ONE...

Then two or more!

Dare to Explore beyond the confines of where the NOW-

Limitations are...

Possibilities that became Probabilities,

By simply TRUSTING that I-

CAN take One Step FORWARD,

Because MY WORLD AWAITS-

ME TO SHOW UP FOR ME!!

While CREATION at its finest WITHIN ME is:

Boldly Personified Harmony,

Notes strummed in the keys of Exuberant Colors,

Vibrantly Woven Together in My Own UNIQUE WAY !!!

< Written: Saturday, 03 November 2018 / 0540 Hours>

"ZEALOUS REFUGE"

Retreat into self,

Take a few moments alone,

Stroll through the park, feed the birds,

Prepare a grand feast for one.

Watch closely, as the sunset caresses the evening Sky,

Going, going, GONE!

The dusk welcomes the Dawn.

The stars rest their heads into the pillows, made of clouds, on the other side of the sun,

Behold! The breaking forth of a New Day comes!

When a Situation lacks-

Motivation and Dedication,

Elevation becomes seemingly Impossible!

May not have as much as some,

But surely have a lot more than others

Be Appreciative at best

Yet never forget where you came from.

Escape to the Future,

Use your Ingenuity and Imagination.

Be thankful for what you have,

Start from where you are with what there is,

Make the absolute best of it all,

That one does with what they already have,

Makes or Breaks the Spirit!

Just because One is Old, do not make them not Wise...

Are you the least bit Surprised??

Embrace each day as if it were the last,

Hope for the Future,

Remember the past,

For it is the past that holds the Keys of Untapped Truth,

Unlocking the Doors of Clarity!

Escape from all that was said and done,

Usually, less was done than - what was Promised and Said--

Yet who shall be able to *Overcome*?

Dance even when there is no music,

But with a song in the heart,

A **WHOLE** is only as great,

As the sum total of the Individual **Parts.**

Not all Broken things are meant to be fixed,

Leave what is dead behind!

Break the shackles and the chains that bind...

Madness and sadness,

Walk away with Dignity in Grace intact,

Waste no more time, Shut the Door,

And Never Look Back!

Walk away from all that sorrow,

Forever can end tomorrow!

Love cell first in most,

Then love others,

Give more to those,

Who are unable to grasp hold their own,

For they lost the way when all their Hope was Gone…

Every shelter that stands is not necessarily a HOME!

<Written: Thursday, 20 May 1999 >

Final Notes:

GRATITUDE and THANKSGIVING

To ALL for traveling along in this GREAT ADVENTURE with me through the Pages of This Book! May you find Peace, Joy, Love, Hope, Renewed Strength, Faith, Perseverance, and Fulfillment in your life.

To get you through the many ups and downs of Life one day at a time, one step at a time, just keep going and never give up!

Thank you for your Generous Support of this project and my works!

Love and Blessings in Abundance to YOU,

Ms. C.K. Ford

ABOUT THE AUTHOR:

Ms. CK Ford- Author, Speaker, Teacher, Mentor, Spiritual Counselor is a native of Louisiana. Currently residing in Atlanta, GA, she has served as an advocate and friend to military veterans' community, at-risk youth, along with being a safe place and voice for those marginalized. Ms. Ford also has served in various aspects of ministry.

Ford – being a Combat Veteran believes that everyone has a purpose, a journey, a path that is unique to who they are. Therefore, she encourages each person she encounters to dig deep in the personal adventure of self-discovery to find their place in the world by allowing their light to shine in who they are as in individual. Every person has value and learning what you bring to the table of life is priceless, thus shall enable you to show up in the Truth, Authenticity, Creativity, and Ingenuity to become the best person that you can be.

Hobbies include reading, writing, cooking, hiking, creating art, and blogging.

For more information and upcoming events, for contact and to book/ schedule me for your event as a Guest Speaker, please make contact through the following channels: Website: www.CKFord.Online

Instagram: CKFord.Online

Facebook: C.K. Ford

Phone: (770) 927-7563

Made in the USA
Columbia, SC
02 June 2021